SCHRÖDINGER'S VAULT

THE FORT KNOX ENIGMA

Crystal Van Wyck Lauer

For all my Pixies—
whose curious minds
never stop asking "Why?"
and whose brave hearts
eternally seek the truth.

PRINTED IN THE UNITED STATES OF AMERICA
ISBN: [TO BE ADDED]
FIRST EDITION

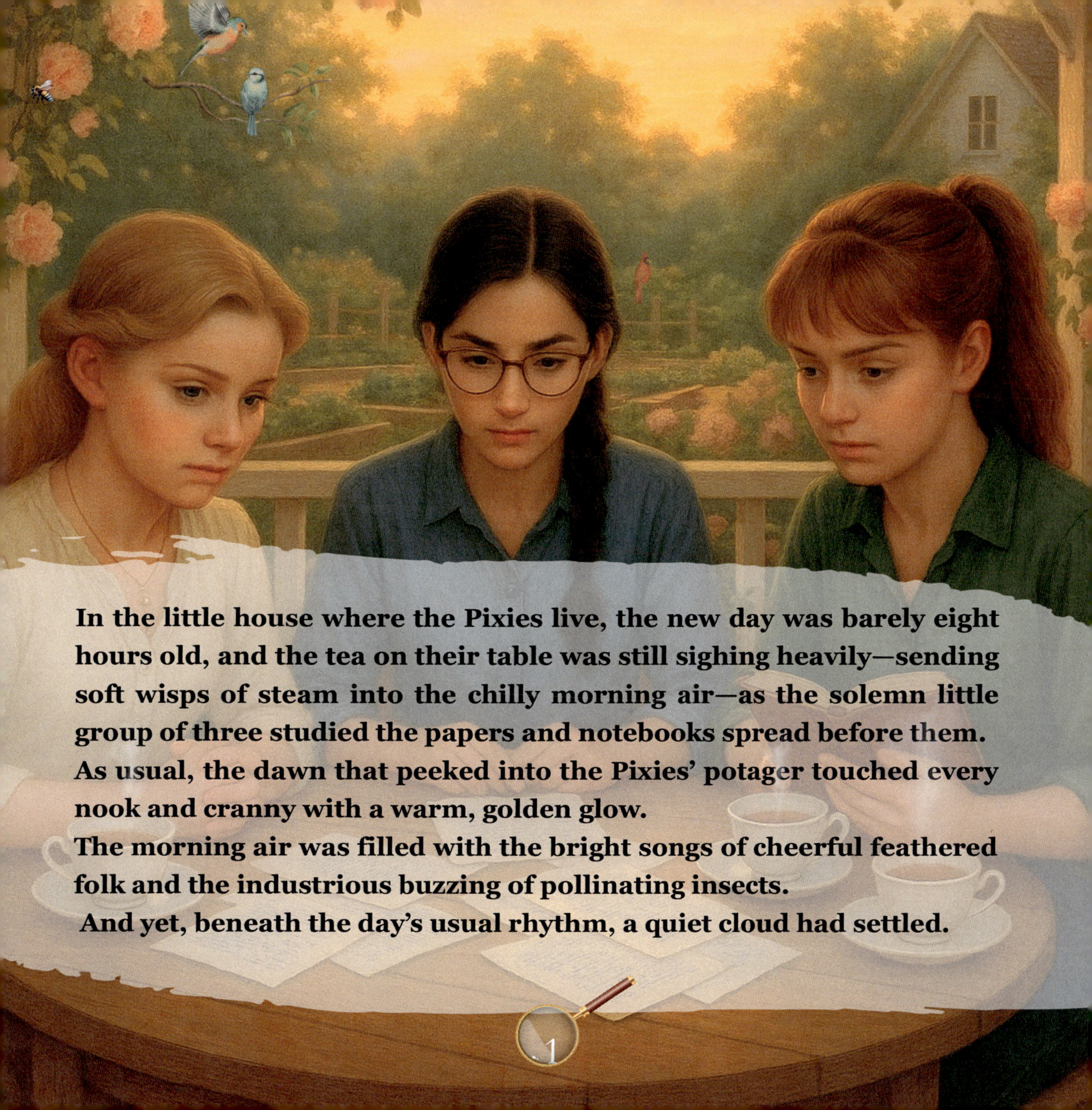

In the little house where the Pixies live, the new day was barely eight hours old, and the tea on their table was still sighing heavily—sending soft wisps of steam into the chilly morning air—as the solemn little group of three studied the papers and notebooks spread before them.
As usual, the dawn that peeked into the Pixies' potager touched every nook and cranny with a warm, golden glow.
The morning air was filled with the bright songs of cheerful feathered folk and the industrious buzzing of pollinating insects.
And yet, beneath the day's usual rhythm, a quiet cloud had settled.

The Golden-Haired Pixie sat deep in thought, her brow furrowed in disapproval, as she and the Dark-Haired Pixie listened with growing concern to the findings the Warrior Pixie had uncovered in their most recent investigation.

So, the President of the United States took everyone's gold?" asked The Golden Pixie, indignantly.

The Warrior Pixie nodded solemnly. "Yes. In 1933, the President ordered all Americans to hand it over—coins, bars, even gold certificates.

In return, they received paper money."

The Golden-Haired Pixie looked appalled.

"They just gave the people paper!" she exclaimed, shaking her head in disbelief at the perceived injustice. "That's some pretty expensive paper!"

The Dark-Haired Pixie nodded in agreement, flipping through the pages of her well-worn notebook.

"The United States Treasury paid everyone $20.67 in paper money for each ounce of gold they turned in," she said quietly.

The Golden-Haired Pixie looked slightly mollified.

"Well... at least $20.67 isn't too terrible," she muttered.

The Dark-Haired Pixie gently interrupted her sister's thoughts.

"But then, not long after—in early 1934—the government raised the official price of gold to $35 an ounce through the Gold Reserve Act. That was after most people had already turned in their gold. They effectively lost about 41% of its new value... and missed out on a nearly 70% increase."

A heavy silence settled over the porch.

Even the birds seemed hushed, as if equally stunned by the news.

The Golden-Haired Pixie's eyes widened—then narrowed in dismay.

"*That* seems pretty tricky," she said.

"I would say so," agreed the Warrior Pixie, her serious hazel eyes scanning the journal in her hands.

"It allowed the government to print more money, but that made each dollar worth less."

"So, people had to pay more... for less," the Dark-Haired Pixie added thoughtfully.

"How could this have happened?" whispered the Golden-Haired Pixie, her fingers drifting to the small cross on the delicate chain around her neck.

"Also, where in the world are the mountains of gold they must have collected?"

The Pixies—who had loved a good mystery, and asking why, ever since they were old enough to speak—leaned in closer, eager to sift through the scattered piles of papers, each one filled with scribbled notes, diagrams, and observations drawn from their careful investigation.

"Ah, here it is!" the Dark-Haired Pixie crowed triumphantly, holding up a single sheet of lined paper, filled front and back with her meticulous handwriting.

"This, I think, is where the story truly begins."

The Golden-Haired Pixie took a sip of her creamy black tea and tucked her feet beneath her, settling more comfortably into her chair.

She would reserve judgment—for now.

The actions of the president, she decided, would need to be carefully examined and thoroughly discussed with her two trusted compatriots before any conclusions could—or should—be drawn.

And so, their tale began, as such things often do, with a foggy morning far away—on a narrow street called Sweeting Alley, in the heart of old London.

There, on October 24th, 1929, a chilling mist crept across the cobblestones, brushing the walls of the London Stock Exchange with curious, wispy fingers.

The stock market is like a giant marketplace—except instead of fruits or vegetables, people are buying and selling tiny pieces of companies, called shares.

When someone buys a share, it means they own a small part of that company. If the company does well, the share usually becomes more valuable. But if the company struggles, the share might lose value.

Inside that grand building, floor brokers—men who buy and sell small pieces of companies on the stock exchange floor for their investors—shouted over one another, their voices thick with urgency.

They didn't notice the fog wrapping around the building outside. They were too preoccupied with the American stocks that were crashing—fast.

Bankers and investors, fearful that the American stock market was about to collapse, began selling everything: railroad shares, utility companies, manufacturers.

By noon, the market floor was an exhausted flurry of motion and panic.

Meanwhile, across the ocean, New York braced for impact. It was still morning there.

Wall Street's traders had barely opened their eyes when the first wave of news about the chaos in the London markets came crashing in.

Brokers rushed to place orders.

Everyone wanted to sell—and no one wanted to buy.

Ticker machines, overwhelmed by the flood of activity, fell behind.

Prices printed on paper lagged behind the market's reality.

No one could keep up. And without up-to-date numbers, people were trading blindly—making decisions without knowing the actual prices.

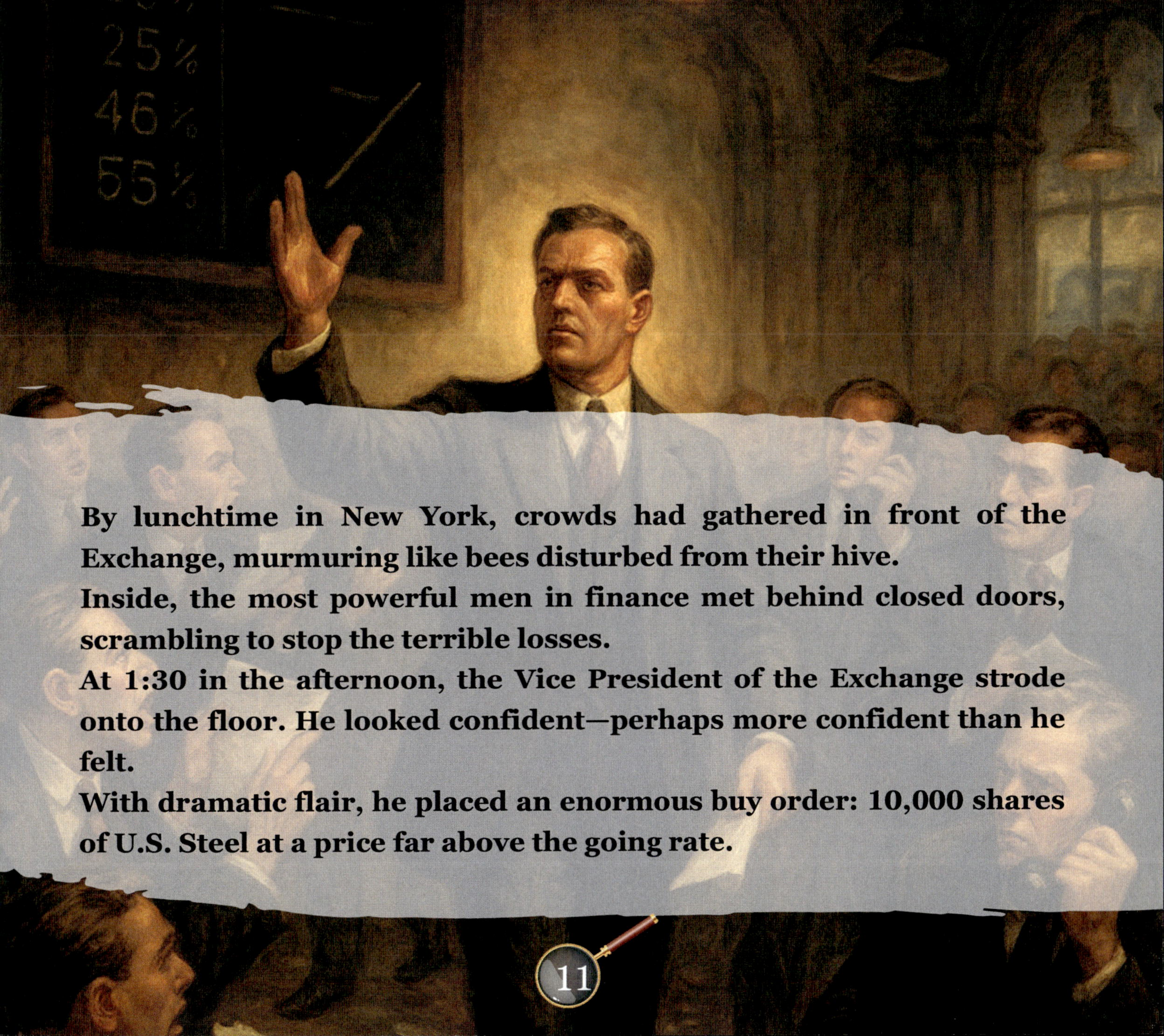

By lunchtime in New York, crowds had gathered in front of the Exchange, murmuring like bees disturbed from their hive.

Inside, the most powerful men in finance met behind closed doors, scrambling to stop the terrible losses.

At 1:30 in the afternoon, the Vice President of the Exchange strode onto the floor. He looked confident—perhaps more confident than he felt.

With dramatic flair, he placed an enormous buy order: 10,000 shares of U.S. Steel at a price far above the going rate.

J.P. Morgan & Co., Chase Bank, and National City Bank had agreed to step in. They bought blue-chip stocks in bulk, hoping to calm the markets and restore order.

It was a message to the people of the country that there was no reason to fear.

Even John D. Rockefeller Jr. made a public statement of faith, buying stocks to show his trust in the American economy.

And for a moment—it worked. The market steadied. The panic paused. People held their breath.

But the damage had already begun. Too many investors had borrowed too much money to make their investments, and now they had to sell even more of their holdings to pay back what they had borrowed.

But the worst was yet to come—five days later, on October 29th:

BLACK TUESDAY

It wasn't just the stock market that fell. It was everything.

By the end of the day, nearly thirteen million shares had changed hands, and fourteen billion dollars in wealth had simply vanished.

Newspapers splashed dramatic headlines across their front pages, and people—fearing their savings would disappear next—rushed to withdraw their money from the banks.

The effects of Black Tuesday rippled outward like circles in a pond. Over the next four years, more than nine thousand banks closed their doors. Businesses collapsed, and one out of every four workers lost their jobs.

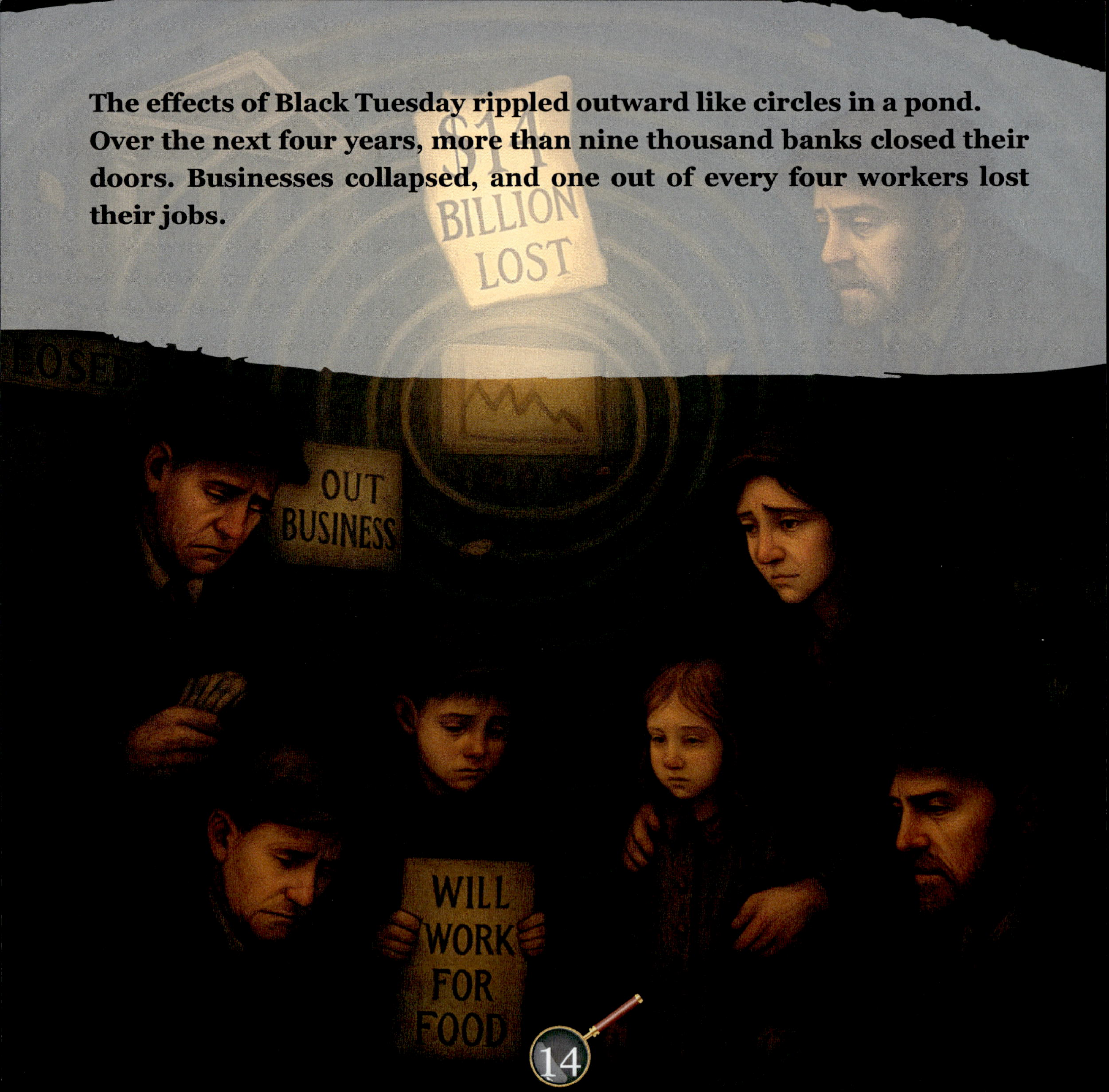

"This was a very dark time in our nation's history," the Warrior Pixie said softly, shaking her head as she set her papers down on the table. The Golden-Haired Pixie and the Dark-Haired Pixie both nodded solemnly.

"Grandpa John's family lost everything in the crash when he was just a little boy," the Dark-Haired Pixie added. "He never forgot it."

She glanced down at her notebook, then continued,

"He said his mother and father had to work wherever they could to make ends meet. They raised rabbits for food and helped in a relative's garden to grow vegetables for their meals."

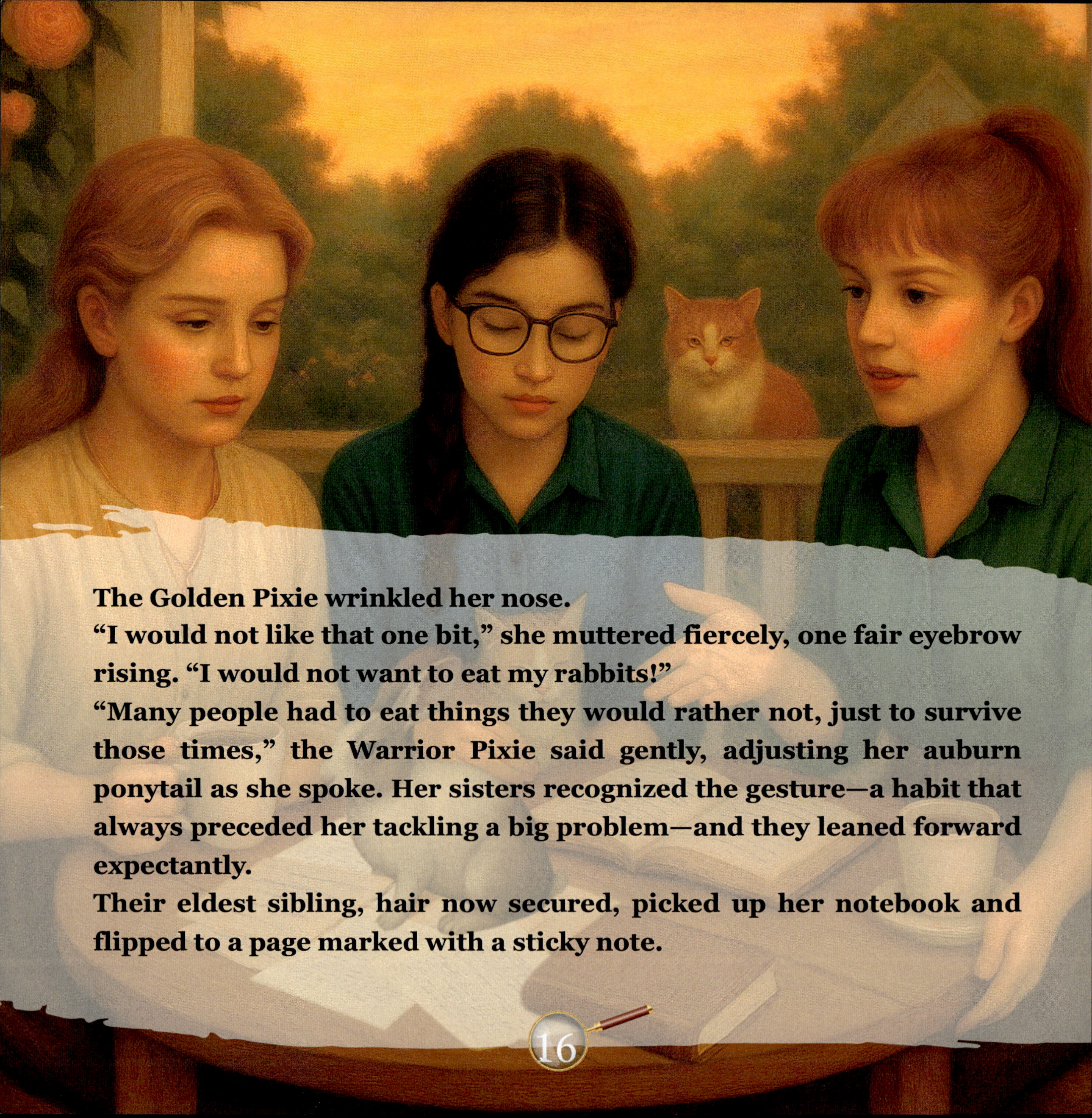

The Golden Pixie wrinkled her nose.

"I would not like that one bit," she muttered fiercely, one fair eyebrow rising. "I would not want to eat my rabbits!"

"Many people had to eat things they would rather not, just to survive those times," the Warrior Pixie said gently, adjusting her auburn ponytail as she spoke. Her sisters recognized the gesture—a habit that always preceded her tackling a big problem—and they leaned forward expectantly.

Their eldest sibling, hair now secured, picked up her notebook and flipped to a page marked with a sticky note.

The Golden Pixie's brow furrowed again.

"But... why did people agree to that?" she asked slowly. "Didn't they question whether the government even had the right to take their gold?"

The Dark-Haired Pixie tapped her pencil against her notebook, her eyes narrowing in thought.

"That's exactly the kind of question we're supposed to ask," she murmured. "What gave the government that authority—and why didn't more people resist?" The Warrior Pixie nodded.

"Most were scared," she said quietly. "It was the middle of the Great Depression. Banks were failing. Jobs were gone. People were desperate... and when fear is high, people sometimes give up more than they realize."

The girls fell silent for a moment—thinking.

"In return, people were handed paper money—promised to be backed by gold," the Warrior Pixie continued. "But not long after, the government raised the price of gold, devaluing the dollar and shifting all the profit to federal control." She paused, her expression tightening. "But that left them with a very big problem."

The Golden Pixie leaned forward, her eyes sharp. "What kind of problem?" she asked.

The Warrior Pixie tapped the page in front of her.

"Well, if the paper money was supposed to be backed by gold—but the gold wasn't allowed to circulate freely anymore—then how could people be sure the paper was still worth anything?"

The Dark-Haired Pixie nodded slowly, her pencil hovering over the page.

"That's the paradox, isn't it? They removed the gold... but told everyone to trust the paper."

For a moment, all three sat in thoughtful silence.

The Golden Pixie wrinkled her nose, sure sign that she was about to ask a question.

"Where do you suppose they put all that confiscated gold?" she murmured, scooping up the curious cat who had wandered too close to her tea, its whiskers twitching indignantly at being thwarted in its mission.

"And that's when President Roosevelt decided to build a fort," said the Dark-Haired Pixie, adjusting her glasses as she glanced back down at her notes. The Golden Pixie blinked.

"That's an odd hobby," she mused, cradling the peeved cat absently as she remembered the forts they'd built from blankets, brooms, and stacks of books. "A bank seems like it would've made more sense."

"It wasn't just any fort," said the Dark-Haired Pixie, typing quickly on her laptop. "It was meant to be the most secure vault on earth. Here it is—Fort Knox. Hidden in the green hills of Kentucky!"

"So secure that even the President needs special permission to enter," added the Warrior Pixie. "And only one ever has—President Roosevelt himself. It's said there are 147.3 million ounces of gold sealed inside."

"So how do we know the gold is still there?" asked the Golden-Haired Pixie. "We don't." Replied the Warrior Pixie. "There hasn't been a full audit since 1953."

The younger Pixies exchanged a concerned glance.

"That's terrible... but what's an audit?" the Golden Pixie asked sheepishly.

"An audit is like a careful checkup," explained the Warrior Pixie. "Someone comes in, examines everything, and makes sure what's supposed to be there... is actually there. For Fort Knox, it would mean opening the vault, counting the gold bars, and confirming that none are missing."

“The people were told the gold was being kept safe for them,” said the Dark-Haired Pixie. “But if no one’s been allowed inside for decades... it’s like a locked treasure chest no one is ever permitted to open.”

“What would happen if someone opened the vault and found out the gold wasn’t there?” the Golden Pixie asked, her voice barely above a whisper.

“That’s the complex part,” said the Warrior Pixie. “It could very well trigger a global economic crisis. The value of money isn’t just about paper and numbers—it’s about trust.”

She glanced at the others, her tone steady.

"If people lost confidence in the currency—if they believed the promises behind it were empty—it could cause panic. Banks might fail. Markets could collapse. The entire financial system depends on people believing that what they're holding has value." The Golden Pixie sat very still.

"So... it's not just about the gold. It's about whether or not we can trust what we've been told."

"Exactly," the Warrior Pixie nodded. "And that's why transparency matters."

"It's like Schrödinger's Cat—only it's Schrödinger's Vault!" exclaimed the Golden Pixie with a grin.

"As long as the vault stays closed, it's both full and empty."

The furry eavesdropper perched on the porch railing paused her morning bath ears twitching at the sound of her favorite word "CAT."

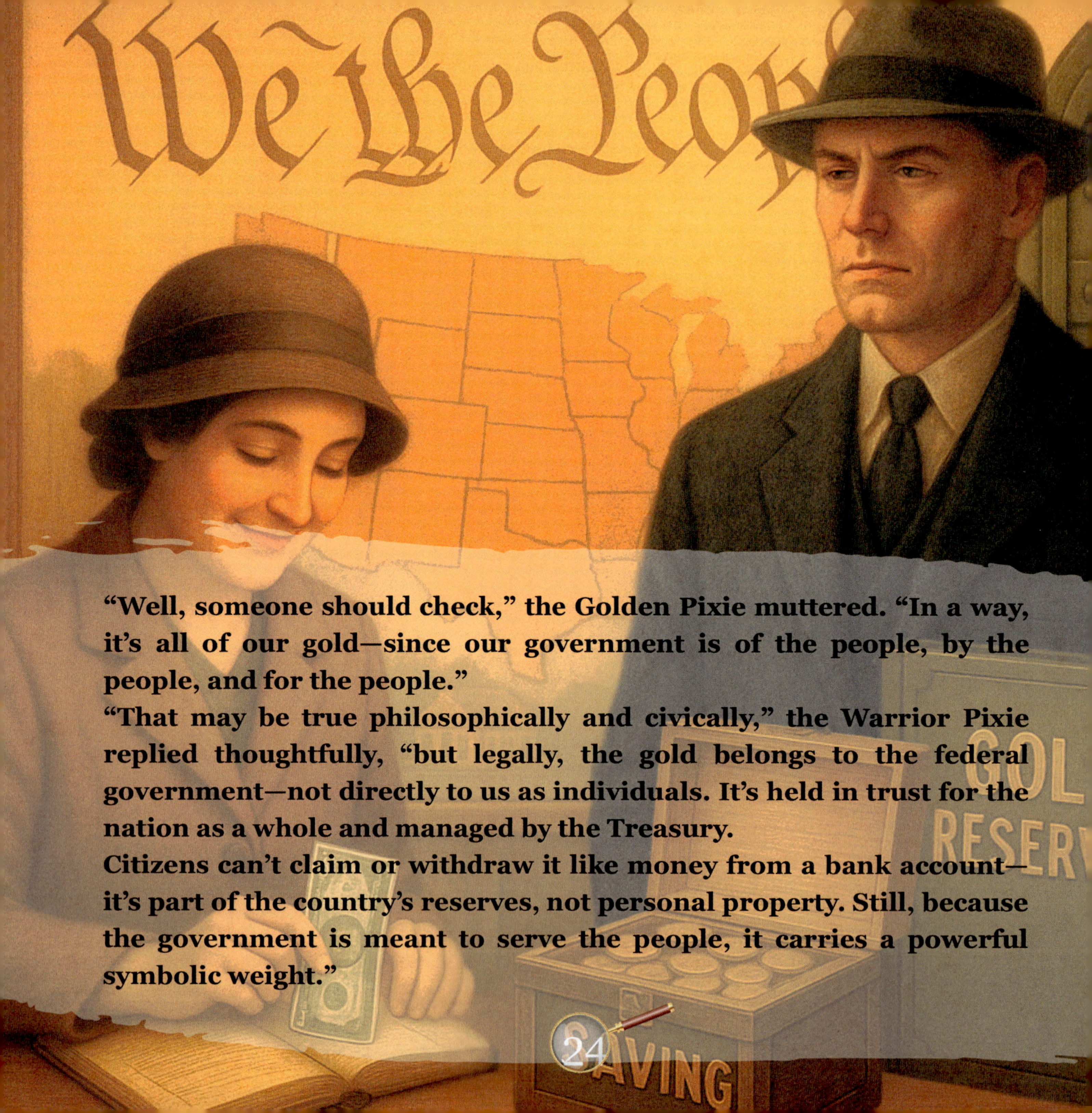

"Well, someone should check," the Golden Pixie muttered. "In a way, it's all of our gold—since our government is of the people, by the people, and for the people."

"That may be true philosophically and civically," the Warrior Pixie replied thoughtfully, "but legally, the gold belongs to the federal government—not directly to us as individuals. It's held in trust for the nation as a whole and managed by the Treasury.

Citizens can't claim or withdraw it like money from a bank account—it's part of the country's reserves, not personal property. Still, because the government is meant to serve the people, it carries a powerful symbolic weight."

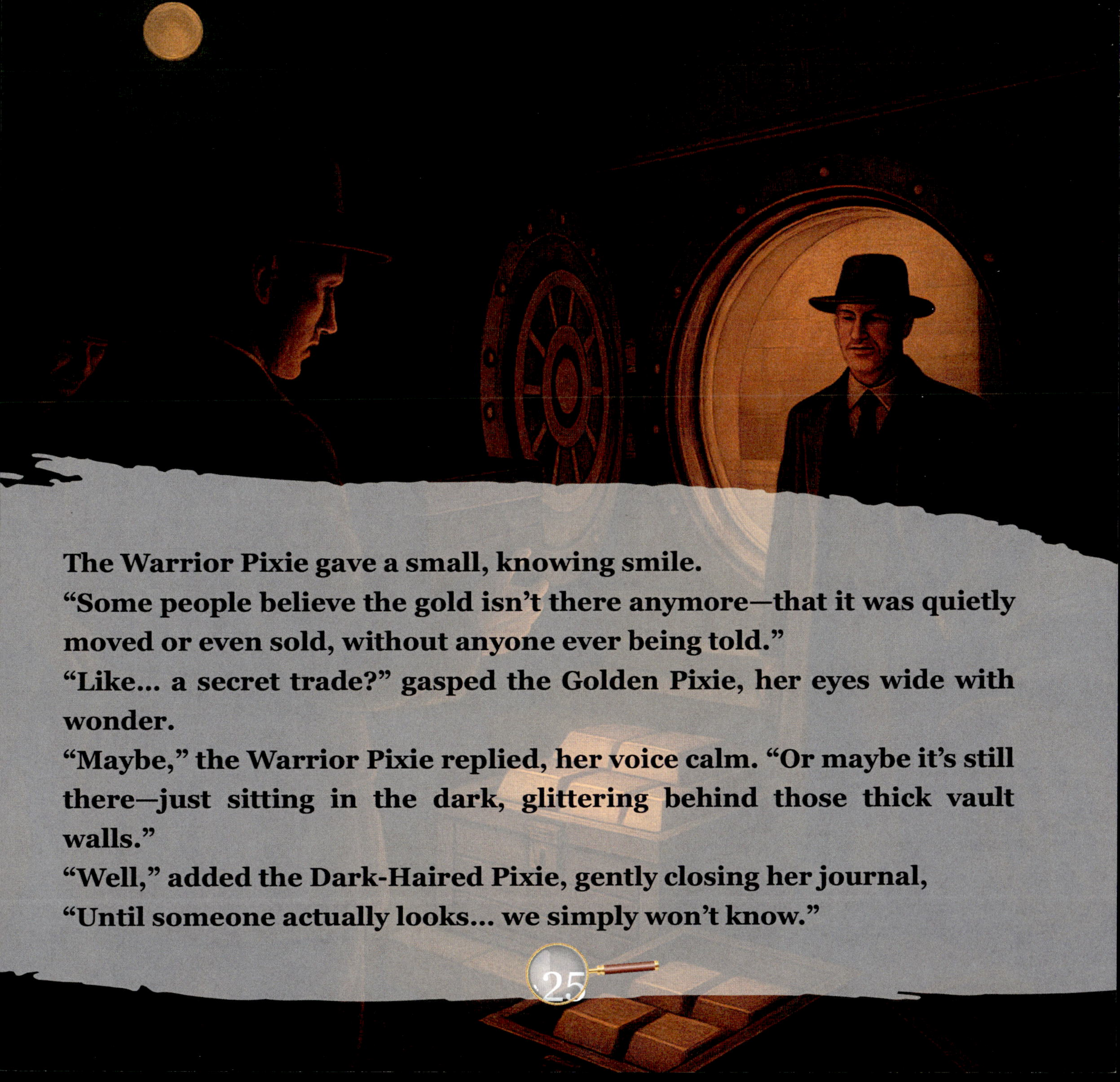

The Warrior Pixie gave a small, knowing smile.
"Some people believe the gold isn't there anymore—that it was quietly moved or even sold, without anyone ever being told."
"Like... a secret trade?" gasped the Golden Pixie, her eyes wide with wonder.
"Maybe," the Warrior Pixie replied, her voice calm. "Or maybe it's still there—just sitting in the dark, glittering behind those thick vault walls."
"Well," added the Dark-Haired Pixie, gently closing her journal,
"Until someone actually looks... we simply won't know."

Silence settled over the porch again—
not one of disbelief this time, but of determination.
In the potager, the breeze rustled the chive blossoms familiarly, and the kettle let out a low sigh of steam, as if even it were thinking.
"We should add this to the Pixie Casebook of Investigations," declared the Golden-Haired Pixie, sitting up straighter in her chair.
"I second that!" said the Dark-Haired Pixie, flipping to a fresh page and writing carefully in her neat hand:
THE GOLD THAT MAY (OR MAY NOT) BE IN FORT KNOX
"And I suggest we keep asking questions," the Warrior Pixie added firmly, "because truth only stays hidden when no one dares to look for it."
Her sisters nodded in agreement as the Dark-Haired Pixie shut the notebook with a crisp snap—
earning a squinty-eyed glare from the now-disrupted feline, who stretched with theatrical drama before leaping off the table in search of a quieter place to nap.

The three Pixies sipped their tea in companionable silence, each deep in thought as the potager sprang to life beneath the doting gaze of the morning sun.

Suddenly, the cat's head reappeared, poking out from the middle of a robust lemon balm bush—giving the illusion that the plant had sprouted a furry, whiskered face. The Pixies burst into laughter at the feline's herbal antics.

"You know," said the Golden Pixie thoughtfully, "I read that cats and dogs can eavesdrop on plants."

"Really?" The Dark-Haired Pixie leaned forward, intrigued, her blue eyes widening.

"Mhmm. When plants are stressed or thirsty, they speak to each other in frequencies we can't hear," the Golden Pixie explained, gesturing toward the lemon balm, which now also sported a sassily twitching tail.

"But cats and dogs can hear it—as well as certain insects and birds," she continued, her voice dropping to a conspiratorial hush.

"I wonder if we could discover how to understand those frequencies —and learn what the plants are actually saying."

The Dark-Haired Pixie immediately opened her notebook as the Warrior Pixie lifted the screen of her laptop.

“After all,” said the Golden Pixie, her eyes gleaming with the excitement of a new investigation, “leafy folk have feelings too...”

The Pixies exchanged a look—one of shared purpose and growing curiosity—thrilled by the certainty that a new investigation was beginning.

Their search for the facts would soon lead them beyond the garden gate and into the forgotten work of a brilliant man named Jagadish Chandra Bose, who, over a hundred years ago, built delicate instruments to listen to the language of plants... and proved that even the quietest living things can feel, respond, and communicate in ways science had never imagined.

But that is a rabbit hole for another day—brimming with gossipy leafy folk, curious frequencies, and scientific secrets springing from the loamy soils of India.

Because knowledge, like science...
is always growing.

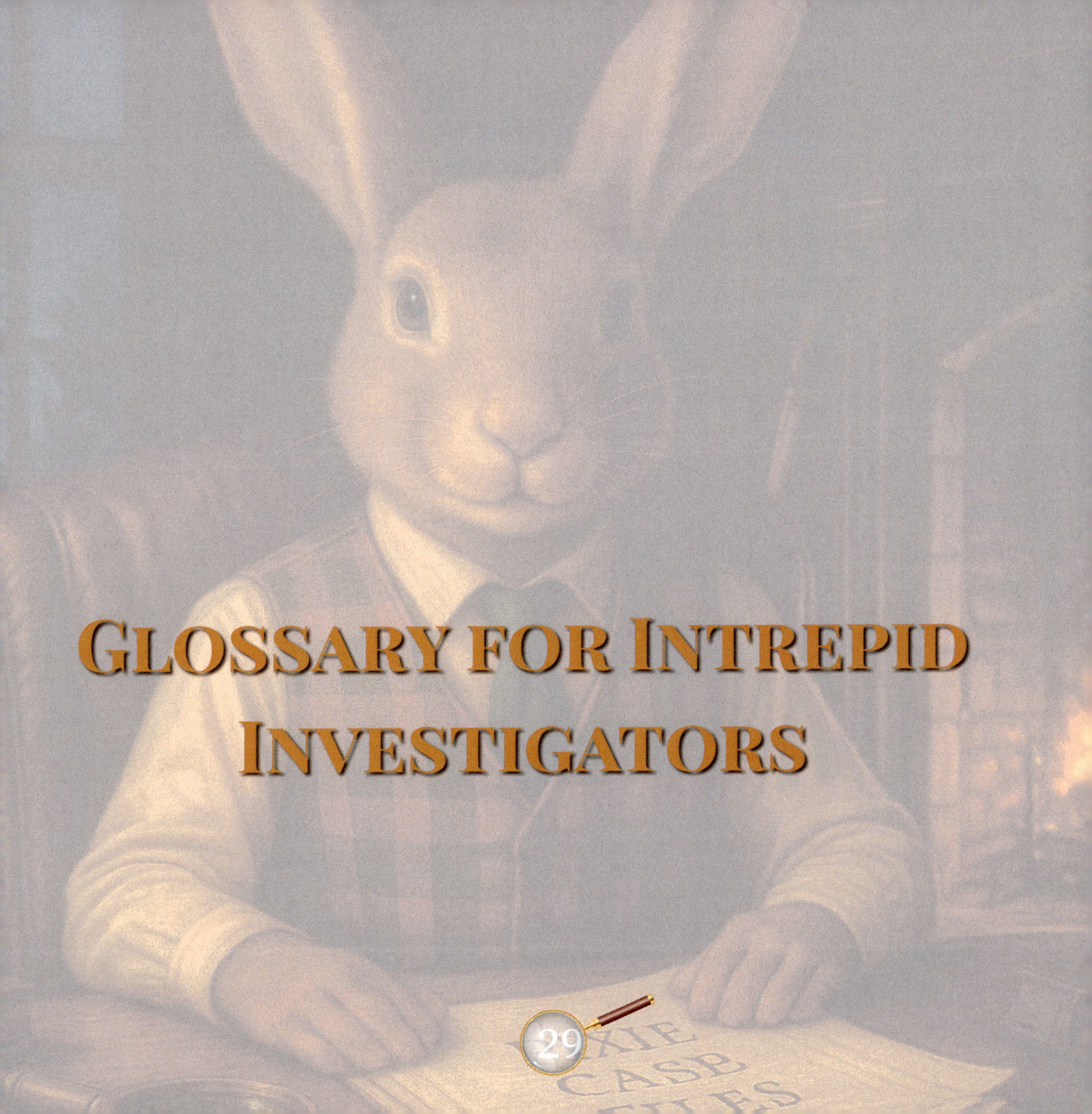

Glossary for Intrepid Investigators

Notable Figures in This Investigation

These real people and powerful institutions played important roles in the events the Pixies explored...

Franklin D. Roosevelt – The 32nd President of the United States who signed Executive Order 6102 and helped lead the country through the Great Depression.

John D. Rockefeller Jr. – A prominent businessman who bought stocks publicly to restore faith in the American economy.

J.P. Morgan & Co., Chase Bank, and National City Bank –Large financial institutions that stepped in during the 1929 stock market panic to try to stabilize the market.

Richard Whitney – The Vice President of the New York Stock Exchange who, during the 1929 crash, dramatically placed a large buy order to restore confidence and calm the markets.

Schrödinger's Cat

(shrow-ding-erz kat)

A *pretend science story to explain how very tiny things work in the quantum world.*

A long time ago, a clever scientist named Erwin Schrödinger came up with a silly-sounding idea to help people understand **quantum mechanics**—the strange rules that tiny invisible things like atoms and particles follow.

He imagined a box with a cat inside. In this made-up story, no one can see inside the box. Until someone opens it, we don't know if the cat is alive or not.

So, in science perception, the cat is in a strange state:
both alive and not alive at the same time!

This is called ***superposition***—when tiny things can exist in two states at once. It's like flipping a coin and, until it lands, imagining that it's both heads and tails at the same time. Don't worry—**no** real cat is ever in trouble.
Schrödinger's Cat is just a thought experiment—a pretend puzzle scientists use to explore how mysterious the tiniest parts of the universe behave.
In the real world, things like cats don't act this way.
Only very tiny things, like **electrons**, do!
But ***Schrödinger's Cat*** helps us imagine how **quantum mechanics** works—by making something invisible... just a little more understandable.

Glossary of Curious Terms for Inquisitive minds

Words are clues that clarify. Even the cleverest mind benefits from keeping a glossary handy. Here are some curious terms that appear in the story. You never know when these terms may be the key to unlocking future mysteries, so study them well—and keep them close in your Casebook of Investigations.

Audit: A formal inspection of records or accounts to ensure accuracy and truth.

Deflation: A decrease in the general price level of goods and services—often makes money more valuable but can hurt businesses.

Executive Order 6102: A 1933 directive from President Roosevelt requiring Americans to turn in their gold.

Fort Knox: A high-security vault in Kentucky built to store the United States' gold reserves.

Gold Reserve Act: A 1934 law that changed the official price of gold and centralized its control.

Shares: Small ownership pieces of a company that can be bought or sold.

Stock Exchange: A marketplace for buying and selling shares in companies.

Treasury: The part of the U.S. government that manages national finances, including gold reserves.

Vault: A secure room or chamber used to store valuable items, like gold.

Made in the USA
Las Vegas, NV
22 October 2025

32780627R00021